Positive Discipline:

A Guide for Parents

2-in-1 Guide on Positive Parenting and Toddler Discipline

Christine Carter

Disclaimer and Terms of Use:
Effort has been made to ensure that the information in this book is accurate and complete, however, the author and the publisher do not warrant the accuracy of the information, text and graphics contained within the book due to the rapidly changing nature of science, research, known and unknown facts and internet. The Author and the publisher do not hold any responsibility for errors, omissions or contrary interpretation of the subject matter herein.
This book is presented solely for motivational and informational purposes only.

Introduction

Hello Supermoms! Welcome to your 2-in-1 guide to effective, positive discipline for children and toddlers. The purpose of this book is to help you teach your little ones safe, growth-promoting behaviors and save you some of the stress and headaches that come with poor discipline. As you move through this book, you will find tips and strategies to help you through some of your child's toughest moments, along with real-world examples and practical advice on staying calm in the face of frustration.

Positive parenting is about so much more than just 'being positive.' It is not about coddling children or ignoring some of life's very real difficulties. It *is* about teaching, guiding, and helping your child to grow in ways that will support healthy behavior from the inside out. Through positive parenting, your child can learn to internalize positive choices and think critically about why self-discipline and healthy behavior are important for their lives.

Parts I and II were originally published as *Positive Parenting: Essential Guide for Parents* and *Toddler Discipline: Essential Guide for Parents*. Now, for the first time, these two guides have been adapted to create this new, more comprehensive overview of positive parenting that's got you covered for every age and stage of childhood. In Part I, we'll go over the basics of what Positive Parenting is all about, discuss some common discipline challenges faced by children at various ages, and give you practical tips, strategies, examples, and more. We know that discipline problems can bring frustration and anger to even the most well-intentioned parents, so you'll also find strategies to help *you* stay calm and parent more effectively and more enjoyably.

Part II moves from the big picture of positive parenting in childhood to a more specific discussion of parenting toddlers. Parenting in the toddler years can be particularly challenging as your little one begins to learn emotional and behavioral self-regulation. Your toddler's cognitive and behavioral development is changing rapidly, and knowing what to expect and how to engage with her through those changes can make a world of difference in supporting her expanding sense of self. Toddlerhood is also an important time for laying the foundations of good discipline and healthy behavior, which can help both your little one and you to have a better experience with discipline during childhood.

If you've never tried positive parenting before, you may find it to be a very different approach than more traditional parenting methods. However, the advantages of positive parenting can have a profound impact on your child's learning and on your experience as a parent. As you move through this book, keep in mind that every family is different. Some of the strategies you find here may be exactly what your child needs, while others may not be right for your specific situation. Don't be afraid to experiment and find what works for your child. If you ever have any questions about a strategy or your child's behavior, speak with your pediatrician.

You may wish to read this book from beginning to end or skip around and read the chapters most relevant to you at a given moment. No matter how you decide to approach these pages, I'm confident that you will find tips, strategies, and perspective to help you in your parenting journey. With conscientious application of positive parenting principles, you too can find increased joy in parenting as you guide your child towards healthy behavior.

Table of Contents

Part 1

Positive Parenting

Introduction: Positive Parenting

Have you ever struggled with getting your child to do his chores? How about convincing her that it's time to come in the house when she'd rather stay outside? From impulse control to emotional regulation to willingness to listen, children struggle daily with learning to function as individuals and members of a family and community. Helping them to navigate that struggle is part of our job as parents – and it can be far from easy! Luckily, the Supermom series is here to help. In this section, you will learn how to promote growth and teach good behavior positively and effectively, while cultivating respect, communication, and healthy boundaries within the home.

The tenets of positive parenting are nothing new, however in recent years they have received increasing attention as researchers around the world have begun to study the benefits of this approach. For today's parent, there is a wealth of resources available on the topic. This guide will help you get started with the basics of positive parenting as well as give you practical tips and strategies for applying it in your home.

There was a time in the not-so-distant past when authoritarian discipline was the norm. Punitive discipline styles were considered necessary for good character development and successful teaching. Rules were crafted and punishments meted out by parents, teachers, and others interested in teaching children how to behave. Obedience to 'the rules' was expected, while disobedience was often met with negative consequences and punishments ranging from painful to uncomfortable to disheartening.

More positive parenting styles are nothing new, and have often coexisted alongside authoritarian parenting styles to some degree. However, today we are seeing more and more families move towards a positive parenting approach, especially as child development research in recent years has consistently shown that a gentler, more positive approach to discipline can be far more effective at cultivating long-term healthy behavioral choices than punitive approaches. Through positive parenting, you can help your child learn to function in your family and community while building a healthy parent-child relationship and creating a safe space for your little one to thrive in as she grows and develops.

This section will address the most crucial and practical aspects of positive parenting, including:

- What is positive parenting?
- How to become peaceful parents
- Tips and strategies for positive parenting

- How to build a connection with your child
- How to communicate effectively
- Common mistakes and how to avoid them
- Alternatives to punishment

The goal is to provide you with the knowledge and tools you need to apply the ideals of positive parenting in real-life scenarios. As you move through the chapters that follow, keep in mind that every child is unique, and even your own child's unique needs and temperament will change as he grows. Some of the strategies presented here may be perfect for helping your little one learn healthy behaviors, while others may not be as useful this week or this year. It may take a little experimentation to figure out what works best for *your* child, but with a little patience, you too can find success with positive parenting.

Let's get started by taking a look at what positive parenting is, and what it isn't.

Chapter 1: Positive Parenting: What It Is and What It Isn't

We've all heard the old lament – wouldn't it be nice if each child came with an instruction manual? Yes, it would be! Unfortunately, that's simply not the way parenting works. Each child is unique, and there is no single, prescriptive set of parenting tactics that works for all kids in all families all of the time. And when it comes to positive parenting, there is no one, single framework of rules that tell us what it means to use positive parenting in the home. Rather, positive parenting can be thought of as a perspective from which parenting choices can be made.

Positive Parenting – What It Is

Put simply, positive parenting is a style of disciplining children that focuses on positive, rather than negative, behaviors and responses. Discipline is focused on finding solutions (rather than punishments) for misbehaviour, recognizing good behavior, and learning for the future rather than punishing negative behavior that has already happened.

Positive parenting fosters mutual respect between parents and children and encourages growth and communication, making them partners in success.

To fully understand positive parenting, an important distinction must be made between *discipline* and *punishment*. Discipline is the process of helping kids learn how to behave and self-regulate. Punishment is one form of discipline that involves giving a negative consequence in response to undesirable behavior. Punishment aims to decrease undesirable behavior by giving children negative experiences physically, emotionally, psychologically, or socially when the misbehavior occurs, so that they will be less likely to repeat the behavior in the future.

In punitive parenting systems, children behave because they are motivated to avoid punishment rather than because they understand the value of positive behavior for their lives. And although punishment can sometimes be used in gentle, healthy ways, in practice it all too often leads to negative consequences for children (and in some cases, outright harm), and can also contribute to parental stress.

Positive parenting, on the other hand, relies on mutual respect and teaching moments to help little ones understand the value of good behavior for their goals, relationships, and development. Children behave because they are motivated to act in ways that encourage positive responses and because they authentically understand and experience the benefits of good behavior.

Positive parenting is characterized by:

Focus on positivity: Positive parenting recognizes and acknowledges a child's good behavior, positive choices, and growing independence in regulating themselves.

Focus on the future: Positive parenting focuses on helping children learn for the future rather than making them 'pay' for what they've done in the past.

Focus on empowerment: Positive parenting seeks to empower children to make their own choices, rather than merely managing children so that they don't misbehave.

Focus on individual strengths: Positive parenting recognizes and draws from the individual strengths, abilities, interests, and desires of a child.

Teaching moments: Positive parenting views discipline and misbehaviour as opportunities for growth and teaching, rather than failures or shortcomings to be punished.

Natural Consequences: Positive parenting recognizes the value of natural consequences to misbehaviour.

Unconditional love: Positive parenting occurs in an atmosphere of unconditional love. In this atmosphere, children feel safe making mistakes, behaviourally or otherwise, because they know that even if discipline occurs, it is not because they are loved or respected any less. When children aren't scared to make mistakes, they are more likely to engage with the world around them and have more learning and growing experiences, further contributing to their sense of empowerment and self-esteem.

Child Centered: Positive parenting is child centered, meaning that parents work as partners with their children to help them construct healthy, productive behaviors, rather than simply handing them a set of rules and expecting them to comply arbitrarily. Parents act as guides, helping children learn for themselves by coaching them through their personal journey of growth and discovery. As children grow, parents help them to learn what behaviors are effective and appropriate for reaching their goals as individuals and succeeding as members of a family, community, and increasingly global world.

Cognitive: Positive parenting isn't just about helping children to approximate a standard of socially acceptable behavior. It also promotes cognitive skills and self-awareness as children learn to make mindful decisions, consider possible outcomes and alternative courses of action, and value and respect themselves and others as agents of choice.

Authenticity: Positive parenting relies on authentic communication between parents and children and focuses on helping a child develop his or her authentic self.

Positive Parenting – What It Isn't

Some may hear the term 'positive parenting' and cringe, envisioning children run wild in a house with no rules, no consequences, and no control. They may think that focusing on the 'positive' will leave children with no coping skills in the face of life's harsh realities, no respect for authority, and no backbone. They may fear that children will become entitled, emotionally weak, or unable to navigate failure.

In fact, the opposite is true! True positive parenting is very effective at helping children learn to be in control of themselves, make good choices, interact with others, and understand the consequences of their actions. So let's dispel some myths about positive parenting by taking a look at what it *isn't*.

Myth 1: Positive parenting means letting kids do whatever they want. Positive parenting does not mean having no boundaries or never telling children 'no.' In fact, positive parenting can involve as many boundaries and 'rules' as other, stricter forms of parenting – the difference is in the response of parents to children who break the rules or who can't have something they want in the moment.

Myth 2: Positive parenting let's kids 'get away with' bad behavior. The problem with the idea of 'getting away with' misbehaviour is that it assumes that children should be punished – that they must somehow pay for their 'crimes.' This philosophy can too easily become reminiscent of the penal system, and often leads to a disconnect between the behavior and the punishment. Positive parenting seeks to reinforce children's understanding of the relationship between behavior and consequence. By focusing on authentic consequences with clearly communicated purposes, children learn how to be more successful in the future rather than paying a penalty for a misdeed.

Myth 3: Moms and dads who use positive parenting are more interested in being friends than parents. Positive parenting does encourage connection, partnership, and even friendship between parents and children.

However, positive parenting is not about sacrificing the role of parent in favour of being best buds with the little guys. Positive parenting is a proactive parenting approach that involves conscientious effort and mindfulness of one's role as a parent who is responsible to teach and nurture children.

Myth 4: Positive parenting fails to teach kids how to handle disappointment and conflict. In fact, positive parenting is an excellent resource for teaching children how to handle disappointment and conflict. Because positive parenting is conscientious, hopeful, and focused on problem solving, utilizing personal strengths, and identifying alternative possibilities, children can learn to put disappointment and conflict into perspective and make choices to help them solve problems or come to terms with alternatives.

Myth 5: Positive parenting means sugar-coating the realities of a child's misbehaviour. Positive parenting does not mean pretending that a child's misbehaviour didn't happen or minimizing the seriousness of a behavioural problem. Rather, it means helping children to recognize the consequences of their actions, learn for the future, and move on. An emphasis on a child's strengths and positive choices does not mean ignoring misbehaviour when it occurs – rather, misbehaviour is seen as a teaching opportunity and a chance to express love and instil hope for the future.

Myth 6: Positive parenting encourages entitlement. Positive parenting does not encourage entitlement – far from it! Positive parenting encourages children to take responsibility for their choices and the consequences of their choices.

Children learn to see the connection between actions and consequences, promoting a realistic, logic-based picture of how the world works.

Myth 7: Positive parenting means praising children all the time. The truth is that positive parenting espouses authentic communication that is delivered respectfully and yes, positively. However, that doesn't mean offering false praise, inflating a child's ego, or praising children 24/7. Children will eventually pick up on praise that is inauthentic or unearned, and when they do, praise begins to lose its value. Positive parenting recognizes this and seeks to praise children authentically, for real accomplishments.

Positive Parenting: An Example

It can be helpful to take a quick look at a real-world example of positive parenting in action.

Mary, a young mother from Nevada, gave her three children, aged 6, 5, and 3, ice cream cones for a snack one afternoon. The oldest, Marissa, became upset when her ice cream fell off the cone onto the table. Distraught, she shoved the blob of ice cream onto the floor, threw her empty cone after it, and began to cry.

At this point, some parents may have responded by yelling at Marissa for making a mess, sending her to her room, giving her a punitive time out, or given her some other form of punishment for throwing her ice cream on the ground. Let's look at how this situation could be handled from a positive parenting approach:

Instead of merely reacting to the sudden mess and angry tears, Mary chose to respond. She got down on Marissa's level and said, 'Man, I hate it when ice cream falls down like that! But we don't need to throw things and cry. That won't help us get more ice cream. Can you try again?'

Marissa calmed down and asked politely for more ice cream, to which Mary responded by dishing some up while asking Marissa to clean up her mess. Mary also praised Marissa for finding an effective, appropriate solution to the problem. Mary then took the teaching moment a step further by asking all three children to work together to come up with ten more ways to solve the problem of ice cream falling off the cone.

They began to giggle and get into the problem-solving activity, with ideas ranging from picking the ice cream up and pushing it down further into the cone, to pre-emptively taping it in place!

In less than 10 minutes, Mary was able to:

- acknowledge and validate her daughter's distress
- point out that the behavior was unhelpful
- help her daughter problem-solve a more successful strategy
- enforce a real-world consequence (cleaning up the ice cream)
- praise her daughter's success
- get all three children involved in a fun, solution-finding activity that helped everyone learn

Through positive parenting, Mary was able to turn a potential tantrum into an opportunity for Marissa to identify and practice good behavior, and for all three children to have fun together and build their relationships.

Who Benefits from Positive Parenting?

The easy answer? Everyone! Children benefit from positive parenting by learning to take ownership of their behavior. As they begin to understand the connection between behavior and real-world consequences, they become empowered as individuals capable of affecting their own reality in ways that make sense. Because positive parenting creates a safe environment for making mistakes, children are able to experiment with the world around them without fear of losing parental love or respect.

Further, because positive parenting relies on good communication and a mutually respectful parent-child relationship, children can experience increased connection and satisfaction with their parents and other family members. Parents benefit from positive parenting for many of the same reasons. They often experience increased connection and satisfaction in their relationship with their child as they work to improve communication and take advantage of teaching moments. Positive parenting encourages parents to respond rather than react, which in turn can give parents a greater sense of control in difficult situations. Positive parenting is effective, which can lead to less stress in the home over time as children learn to behave appropriately.

Communities also benefit from positive parenting. Children who grow up in positive environments of unconditional love, emotional safety, and personal empowerment are less likely to experience depression, substance abuse, and unemployment as adults. They are also more likely to pass adaptive behaviors on to their children when they have their own families.

As you can see, positive parenting has many benefits. However, this isn't a one-size-fits-all approach. As discussed earlier, positive parenting is a perspective rather than a prescription. There are many techniques and strategies that can be applied from this perspective, and not all of them will be right for your child. We'll get into some of these practical applications soon, but first, let's set the stage by discussing how to become a peaceful parent.

Chapter 2: Steps to Becoming a Peaceful Parent

Becoming a peaceful parent is not always an easy task. The demands of modern life can mean that parents are already under stress, deadlines, and pressures even before children are thrown into the mix. Some days, it can feel like our kids are testing the limits of our patience to the breaking point.

The truth is that when we're angry, we tend to react rather than respond. Depending on the situation, reacting may put a quick stop to misbehavior, but it rarely allows for teaching moments to occur. Reacting leads to yelling, ordering children to their rooms, in-the-moment punishments, and often overlooks or ignores teaching opportunities. It's also stressful for parents! Too much anger can make parenting unenjoyable and leave you feeling out of control.

Even the most practiced of parents will have moments when calm seems far away and anger flares. In the face of these moments, it's all too easy for positive parenting strategies to go out the window. The question becomes, how can we manage our anger and stay calm so that positive parenting can take place?

Patience Is Vital – Tips and Techniques to Stay Calm in Critical Situations

Let's take a look at some mindful strategies for staying calm, finding patience, and responding rather than reacting:

1.   *Make a commitment to yourself.* This is not an instant-fix tip, but it does help. Making a formal commitment to yourself that you are not going to lose your temper won't stop it from happening ever again – but over time, this consciously made commitment can help you to be more aware of what's going on situationally and internally when you lose your temper. As you gain insight into your own feelings and the parenting situations that bring them on, you can start to make more mindful choices in those frustrating moments. Don't give up. As you begin to notice your anger and become better at managing it, the effectiveness of your parenting can increase. As that increases, your child's misbehaviour will start to decrease. Decreased misbehaviour means less stress, which leads to less anger. In other words, consistently being mindful of your frustration over time can lead to a happy snowball of more enjoyable parenting!

2.   *Put it in perspective.* It can be all too easy to start worrying when children test boundaries, push buttons, or misbehave. It's not uncommon for over stressed parents to start asking questions like, 'Why are they doing this? Is it because I'm not a good parent? Am I failing somehow?' Before you know it, things have escalated to 'What if they NEVER learn? What if they end up living under a bridge?!' Try to calm down and remember that button-pushing, boundary testing, and misbehaviour are all normal. They are a healthy part of your child's attempts to experiment with and understand the world around her. Expect that these things will happen. Recognize that your job is not to eliminate such issues overnight, but to guide your children through the process of growth and discovery that comes with learning how to function safely and healthily in the human condition. That being said, if you are worried that your child's behavior is outside the norm, seek specific guidance from your pediatrician.

3.   *Take a deep breath.* Sounds simple, doesn't it? Believe it or not, taking a moment to breathe is more than just pat advice. A few calming breaths can be done in under thirty seconds, but do wonders for helping you calm down. Deep breathing delivers oxygen to your blood and brain, which can help you relax and think more clearly under stress. The few seconds or minutes you spend doing this exercise can also give you a chance to pause and collect yourself before you react. You may even want to ask your children to breathe with you.

4.   *Splash water on your face.* Taking a moment to splash cold water on the face helps some people to change their internal landscape just enough to step away from the anger. However, only apply this strategy, or any strategy that requires you to step away from your children, if it is safe to do so.

5.   *Add new tools to your toolbox.* Come up with a list of anger management techniques that have worked for you in the past, then go out and find some new ones to add to the list (hint: this chapter is a great place to start!). When you feel anger coming on, pull one of these 'tools' from your anger management toolbox. Simply being prepared with options when things escalate can do wonders for one's ability to regain control.

6.   *Remember that feelings are contagious.* If you are angry, anxious, or stressed, your children probably will be too. Kids are smart – even when parents control their reactions, it's likely that little ones will pick up on the fact that mom or dad is upset. This can stress children out and lead to further misbehavior, adding fuel to the fire. Taking a moment to remember that our own anger is making things worse can sometimes give us the pause we need to apply a calm-down strategy.

7.   *Tip 4: Take a break.* Sometimes taking a short break can give you the space you need to regain your calm. This strategy can even be turned into a teaching moment as you model a healthy coping technique for your child. If you feel that you just can't keep it together, tell your children that you are upset and you need to take a break to calm down. Then leave (providing it is safe to do so), take

a quick walk, run through some breathing exercises, do some yoga poses – whatever helps you calm down best. When you return, you can ask your children why they thought you needed a break and jump into a teaching moment around coping with difficult emotions.

How to Stop Yelling at Your Child

A common but unfortunate side effect of anger is yelling. While yelling can sometimes put a stop to misbehavior in the moment, it's less effective in the long run for promoting discipline. It can also undermine parent-child relationships, create stress for everyone involved, and interfere with authentic attempts at communication. That being said, it's probably not the end of the world if you yell at your kids one day. It happens in most families from time to time, and beating yourself up over it is usually not helpful. Just as you want to teach your kids to learn from their mistakes and move on, if you yell at your child, learn from the experience, make amends, forgive yourself, and then move on so that positive parenting can take effect.

It should be noted that in this chapter, we are not discussing the yelling that is sometimes necessary in safety situations, such as warning your child to get out of the road in the face of an oncoming vehicle. The focus here is on yelling as the result of anger, or other negative emotions.

Let's stock up that peaceful parent toolbox a little more by looking at some tips and tricks to stop yelling:

1. *Ask your kids to explain their feelings.* It can be easy in a heated moment to feel like your child is acting out just to make you angry. Understanding the real reasons

why a child has misbehaved can help add a little perspective and cool the fuse of our own anger.

2.   It's also good for kids, who need to be heard and validated at least as much as adults do. Just listening to your child's feelings may be enough to reduce the misbehavior, which will in turn help your frustration levels.

3.   *Get a stress ball.* Many people swear by these small devices. Having a stress ball to squeeze can give you something else to focus on when you're about to lose your cool, and the physical use of your hands can help take the edge off of your stress. You can try keeping one in your bag and pulling it out in heated moments.

4.   *Don't take it personally.* Know that your child's misbehavior is not personal. Misbehavior is a normal part of development and to be expected as she learns to self-regulate her actions and emotions. Taking it personally will not only add to your stress in the moment, it can also lead to resentment over time.

5.   *Disengage.* Until you can calm your anger, do nothing. If you've already started yelling, stop where you're at. Take a moment to calm down before you resume the interaction. The more often that you stop yourself, the more quickly you'll be to notice that you're yelling. Eventually, this strategy can help you avoid yelling altogether.

6.   *Don't force a teaching moment.* Positive teaching moments can't happen when you're yelling. Wait until you've calmed down before trying to teach your child.

7.   *Take preventative action.* If you know that having the plant knocked over sets you off, put it out of reach. If you know that your children's' fighting over a particular toy will lead to your yelling, put the toy away until they are ready to play without fighting. If you know that going home from the park will lead to yelling if your children refuse to come home, make a plan for how you will deal with their refusal in a more constructive way. Identifying situations that lead to yelling can help you eliminate them when appropriate and plan personal coping strategies when not.

8.   *Set realistic expectations.* Frustration is more likely to occur when your kids fail to meet the behavioral expectations you've set for them. Setting expectations that are too advanced for their developmental level will only lead to 'failures' on their part and frustration for both of you. Give them – and yourself – plenty of opportunities to succeed by setting behavioral expectations that are in keeping with their developmental level.

Chapter 3: Tips for Positive Parenting

Now that we've discussed what positive parenting is (and isn't) and set the stage with some great tips for staying calm in the face of misbehavior, it's time to move on to some practical positive parenting tips! These strategies are a great addition to the parenting toolbox, and can be pulled out as situations arise. Don't be afraid to experiment with these techniques, and keep in mind that your child is unique. Not everything will work for everyone, but at the very least these ideas can act as a jumping off point for finding your own blend of effective positive parenting strategies.

1. Look for the root cause. Positive parenting is largely about problem-solving. Understanding why your child has misbehaved can help you to identify the most effective strategy for a particular discipline problem. For example, if your child has colored in her brother's book because she can't find any paper, you will probably respond and teach differently than if she's done it out of anger after a sibling conflict. However, you can't make that decision if you don't know what's causing the behavior.

2. Be kind but firm. Success in positive parenting is all about balance. Be too passive with your children and discipline problems are likely to increase. Cross the line into aggression, and you have the same problem. The trick is to be kind but firm as you discipline your child. Use a firm tone, make eye contact, and be consistent as you enforce rules. Avoid yelling, angry faces, and harsh body language. Doing so will help your child to realize that rules and consequences are consistent, predictable, and present for reasons other than anger or retribution.

3. Acknowledge your child's feelings. An important component of the positive parenting philosophy is the idea that your child's feelings are important and worth listening to. When your little one misbehaves, take a moment to check in with her and find out how she's feeling. Validate her feelings while remaining calm, but firm, and continue to enforce the boundary.

For example, one day Trinity asked her seven-year-old, Clarie, to stop playing with her toys because it was time to help with the family chores. Clarie didn't want to stop playing, so she became upset and began to whine.

Instead of insisting that Clarie stop and threatening consequences, Trinity took a moment to acknowledge her daughter's feelings. She got down on Clarie's level and said, 'It looks like you're having a really good time. Are you enjoying playing right now?' When Clarie nodded, Trinity smiled. 'That's great! I can see that you've got a really fun story happening with your dolls. It must be disappointing to take a break right now.'

Then, having acknowledged Clarie's feelings, Trinity took a moment to teach and reinforce the boundary: 'It's kind of hard to take a break in the middle of something fun, but you know what? We can do hard things, because we're super strong.' Clarie, who now felt understood, important, and believed in, got up and went to do her chores.

This strategy won't always go this smoothly, but it often helps. And even when it doesn't, acknowledging your child's feelings will help her to feel understood, adding to the emotional bank account for future interactions.

4. Be consistent. Consistency is key with many aspects of parenting. For positive discipline, it's vital. Once a rule or boundary has been established, consistently sticking with that rule will help your child learn that it will always be enforced. It will also help them to practice the skills they need to keep the rule and give them the reassurance of knowing what is expected of them.

5. Communicate expectations. Let kids know what the expectations are and what the consequences of violating rules will be. When they know what to expect, they are better able to make behavioural choices. Kids need structure and predictability. Communicating and then consistently following through with expectations is an important part of providing that.

6. Learn. Update your understanding of positive parenting by actively learning. This book is a great place to start. The CDC also has some excellent free videos and interactive activities about positive parenting.

Additionally, you may want to check into positive psychology, a branch of psychology that deals with how people experience happiness and what gets them there.

7. Time out. Time outs are a time-tested consequence for misbehavior. However, they can be either positive or punitive depending on how they are approached. To use time outs positively, don't treat them as a punishment or negative consequence. Instead, treat them as a tool for helping your child learn to cope. Positive time outs remove your child from whatever is contributing to their misbehavior so that they can cool down and regroup. Positive time outs should be given in a comfortable, safe place. Your child should know why they are in time out and the purpose of the time out – usually to give them time to cool down and relax so that they can be more successful, and not as a punishment. After the timeout is over, you can discuss with your child why they needed a time out, how it helped, and what they can do differently in the future to avoid needing one again.

8. Look for learning opportunities. This one can't be stressed enough. One of the greatest advantages of positive parenting is the focus on learning opportunities. Learn to watch for chances to teach your little one valuable life lessons, from in-the-moment behavioural lessons such as not hitting to big-picture concepts such as the importance of building healthy, happy relationships.

9. Be patient. Parenting in general requires a good dose of patience, but positive parenting may require a bit more than some other methods.

Yelling, threats, and harsh punishment can sometimes stop misbehavior more quickly in the moment, but they miss out on the opportunity to help children grow for the future. Acknowledging feelings, taking advantage of learning opportunities, and problem-solving root causes with your child does take a little more time, but it's usually more effective in the long run – not to mention better for your child's growth and development and for your relationship with him.

10. Start early. It's never too early to start using positive discipline! Even babies and toddlers can benefit from gentle, developmentally appropriate guidance towards healthy, successful boundaries and behaviors. Remember, positive parenting is much about teaching opportunities, and your toddler can benefit from this just as much as an older child. Starting early can also help ease your growing baby into the challenges of childhood discipline with less stress for both you and her. Check out the Supermom Series book on toddler discipline to get an in-depth look at how to use positive parenting with little ones aged 1-3 years.

11. Be playful. Try turning sticky situations into games. For example, if your four-year-old doesn't want to pick up his toys, challenge him to a contest to see if he can pick them up before the end of an exciting song, or play a friendly game of 'chase' with a stuffed lion that wants to eat all of the toys that aren't in the bucket. Songs, chants, games, and challenges can turn a frustrating situation into fun for both you and your child. It also helps your little one to succeed in meeting an expectation and experience the confidence and empowerment that comes from success.

12. Create opportunities for success. Create rules and consequences that are developmentally appropriate. Setting expectations too high for your child's age only sets them up for failure and frustration. Give her choices and expectations that she can succeed with, to bolster her confidence and promote self-empowerment. The more that your child is used to succeeding with behavioural expectations, the easier it may be for him to continue the trend as new rules are introduced.

13. Use distraction. Sometimes, particularly with young children, a distraction can diffuse a frustrating situation and help you to avoid a tantrum. Tantrums are a normal part of life for toddlers and very young children, but if they happen often then your child may be spending more time in a negative head space than is necessary. It can be hard to teach good choices when little ones are feeling upset. Sometimes, it's better to offer a distraction to stop the misbehaviour and move on in a more positive way, especially if your child is still a toddler.

14: Focus on good behavior. Catch your child being good! Look for things he does well and take the opportunity to give authentic praise. Reward good behavior with smiles, hugs, high-fives, and even formal rewards such as extra play time. Don't give out praise tritely or when it isn't deserved, but do find ways to focus on your child's good behavior and let them know how awesome you think they are.

Chapter 4: How to Build a Connection with Your Child

Applying the tips in chapter 3 is much easier to do when you already have a good connection with your child. Positive parenting promotes mutual respect and loving relationships, so building a connection with your child is important. However, it's not always easy to maintain!

For many, modern life is filled with distractions, competing priorities, and too little time. All of these things can get in the way of building and maintaining a strong connection with our family members, including our children. Once they hit kindergarten, they may spend the better part of their days at school and afterschool activities, or friends' houses, while we may be working long hours or fighting to make enough time for all of the important people in our lives, including our children. Without conscientious effort, connections can suffer and family relationships become harder.

A positive connection with your child can help foster their sense of security, independence, and love. It's also satisfying. The parent-child connection can and should be pleasurable to both sides of the relationship, even though both will inevitably experience frustration as well.

In terms of positive parenting, your connection with your little one will help you to be more sensitive to their needs so that you can make better decisions about positive discipline. It will also help you to cultivate a sense of trust with your child, encouraging growth as they feel free to ask for help and experiment in safe spaces.

How you connect with your child – and what that connection looks like – will vary based on their age and developmental progress. Let's take a look at some helpful tips and suggestions for building connection with your little one depending on their age and developmental level. Keep in mind that not everything listed here will work for every child, and some strategies can be applied at more than one stage of development. If you find that a particular suggestion doesn't make sense for your family right now, simply set it aside. It may be useful down the road when your child is older or in a different phase of life.

Age	Social/Emotional Development	Tips for Connecting
1-2	• Increased independence • Begins to show interest in new people • Begins to show defiant behavior • Imitates the behavior of others, especially adults and older children • Begins to form simple phrases and sentences • Follows simple instructions and directions	• Play simple games together • Read to your toddler • Talk to her, including asking her to find things or name body parts and objects • Respond to wanted behaviors more often than you punish unwanted behaviors • Encourage him to explore and try new things • Take field trips together, such as going to the park • Sing to her • Give lots of hugs and cuddle time
2-3	• Imitates the actions of others • Express a wide range of emotions • Engages in imaginative play • Shows affection for others • Begins to engage in turn-taking	• Play pretend with your child • Go exploring together with a walk or wagon ride • Encourage your child to tell you his name and age • Learn simple songs

		• behaviors • Shows concern for others in distress • Understands possession, such as 'mine' vs 'his' • Displays a wide range of emotions • Increased independence and willingness to explore without a parent's presence	• and rhymes together • Play parade or follow the leader • Give praise for following instructions, positive behavior, and good choices • Make story reading interactive by asking questions about what she sees in the pictures
3-5		• Becomes increasingly creative with imaginative play • Engages imaginative play with other children • Enjoys playing with other children more than playing alone • Can tell the difference between what's real and what's make-believe more often, but not always • Is able to cooperate sometimes • Talks about likes and interests • Increased interest	• Do simple chores together • Ask your child to recount what they did during the day and what they liked or didn't like about particular activities • Give your child choices • Build simple puzzles together • Make things together: color pictures or do age-appropriate crafts • Sing songs with gestures • play more complex games together • Be engaged with preschool and

		in people outside the family • Wants to please others • Increased independence • Increased requests for information as they explore • Becomes aware of gender • Remembers short stories and songs	kindergarten activities and homework • Have 'date nights,' special outings for one-on-one time with mom or dad • Praise her for good behavior, focusing on things she can control (such as choosing to help a sibling) over things that she can't control (such as being smart)
6-8		• Increasing independence and confidence when away from parents and family • Thinks about the future. • Understands the concept of roles • Friendships become more important • Can engage in more teamwork • Wants to be liked by friends • Uses increasingly complex language to talk about their own thoughts and feelings • Shows empathy and concern for	• Recognize accomplishments in school and activities by praising work well done and displaying it in the home • Talk with her about things she looks forward to • Talk with her about her friends and school • Do kind things together, such as baking cookies and taking them to a neighbour • Attend fun events together - movies, community events, and

	others	festivals • Take turns reading to each other; when your child reads, ask questions about the story and help him make connections to his life • Continue to praise good behavior and choices
9-11	• Attention span increases • Begins to engage in more complex relationships with friends and • Relationships with friends becomes more emotionally important to have friends • Starts to experience greater peer pressure • Greater independence from parents and family • Can more clearly see the point of view of others	• Learn something new together • Ask your child to teach you something they learned at school • Spend time together • Ask about her friends • Ask about her accomplishments challenges • Involve him in helping to make plans for the family, such as planning meals together or setting family goals • Acknowledge and appreciate accomplishment • Continue to make room for one-on-

		one time and 'date nights,' even though he is becoming increasingly interested in spending time with friends

*Adapted from information found at www.cdc.gov.

In addition to the above age-specific tips, let's take a look at some general suggestions for building connections with your children. Some of these suggestions will help you to create a family environment in which connection can occur, while others are concrete, practical activities you can do with your child to build your connection together.

1. *Make family relationships important.* Teach your children that family relationships are important and valuable. Verbalize this importance often and reinforce their awareness of themselves as valued members of a family by creating meaningful family traditions, structures, and routines. Make sure to let them know how important they are to the family and how happy you are to have them there.

2. *Interact on their level.* Make eye contact, get down on the floor with your child, play games that he enjoys, have conversations about things he's interested in. Children can experience a more meaningful connection with you when they feel that you are interested in what they are and when the interaction occurs in ways that they can understand and relate to.

3. *Show affection.* Don't be shy with smiles, hugs, and positive words. Let your child know that you enjoy being

around them, that you take pleasure from their presence in your family, and that you value them. Focus on things that you genuinely like about them, so that they know you love them not just because you're their mother, but also because you enjoy them as people.

4. *Apologize*. If you make a mistake, model the behavior you would like your children to learn. Don't be afraid to acknowledge the mistake or apologize for it. Doing so can help build a sense of mutual respect between you and your child.

5. *Pay attention*. It's all too easy get focused on our smartphones, what we're planning for dinner, or the meeting we have at work tomorrow. Sometimes this can't be avoided, but try to put such distractions aside during conversations with your child and give them your full attention. Use active listening to engage with them and show that you value what they have to say.

6. *Play together*. Children love to play, and playing with them can be a great opportunity to build connection and add to the emotional bank account. Engaging in games like chase, hide and seek, or even getting on the floor to play with toys together will build up positive experiences between you and your child and can be full of opportunities for positive teaching if you look for them.

7. *Read stories together*. Many children find it calming to sit next to mom or dad and read stories together. Story time can build connection by giving you and your child a chance to share an imaginative experience together. Enhance the experience by asking questions about pictures and ideas from the story, making predictions together, and extending story evens and concepts to your child's real life.

Chapter 5: How to Stay United and Communicate Effectively

A healthy connection isn't the only important factor in effective positive parenting. Unity and effective communication are also key components of a healthy, growth-promoting home environment and parent-child relationship. Good communication helps parents and children to understand each other, to express needs, to share thoughts, feelings, and perspectives, and to work together to problem-solve difficult or frustrating situations.

Active listening is a great place to start for positive communication. Active listening is just what it sounds like – listening that is active. The following active listening skills can help you and your child to communicate more effectively:

1. Get rid of distractions. Active listening starts when you focus on your child with your full attention. Make sure to set aside distractions, such as smartphones or laundry, so that you can listen fully and attentively.

2. Make eye contact. Eye contact lets your child know that you are listening.

3. Be aware of facial expressions. While there's no need to paste a fake smile on your face, try not to look impatient or bored while your child is talking. If you are feeling impatient or bored, take a breath and try listening even more actively. Try to understand everything your child is telling you – there is a lot you can pick up on from a child's communication, beyond the words they use.

5. Use body language. Show that you are listening by facing your little one, leaning slightly forward, and nodding at appropriate times.

4. Paraphrase. Paraphrase what your child has said to make sure that you understand their meaning and to let them know that you are listening and want to understand. Use phrases like, 'Do you mean that you …?' or 'It sounds like you …. Is that right?'

5. Acknowledge feelings. Acknowledge feelings that are expressed. If appropriate, help your child to express their feelings with phrases like, 'That sounds difficult. How did you feel about that?'

Again, active listening is a great place to start when it comes to communicating with your child. Additionally, the CDC has recommended the following three keys to communication:

1.   Praise your child when she does something right. The more you praise a behavior, the more likely it is your child will behave the same way again.

2.   Pay attention to your child when he is talking to you or trying to communicate with you. Giving him your full attention will help you understand what he is telling you. It will also make him feel like you care about what he has to say.

3.   Set aside time each day to talk and play with your child. Creating a special time lets your child know she is important. It also strengthens the bond between the two of you.

When it comes to positive parenting, an important part of communication is helping your child to understand the purpose of discipline and good behavior. Teaching your child *why* good behavior is important, and why you discipline them, can help them to see you as their partner in success.

As you problem solve situations together, taking a moment to communicate how proud you are of their efforts to succeed and how important their contribution to the problem-solving process is can increase the sense of unity that they feel with you. Giving them choices in their own discipline can also help them to feel that you are working with them, as a unified team trying to reach a goal, rather than against them as an external force that must be appeased.

Chapter 6: Common Mistakes and How to Avoid Them

Every parent makes mistakes. Luckily, knowledge can go a long way towards minimizing them, not to mention saving you and your kids time and stress! Even the most well-intentioned moms and dads can't avoid mistakes if they don't know what they look like. Let's take a look at some common positive parenting mistakes and how to avoid them:

1. *Inconsistency.* There's no denying that sometimes, it's easier to give up or give in than to engage through positive parenting. And it's not always about yelling to put a quick stop to misbehavior, either. When four-year-old Jon wouldn't stop whining about a second snack, his mother, Bethanne, began to get frustrated. She was tired, she had a headache coming on, and she wanted

to focus on getting the bills payed. She had tried to enforce the 1-snack rule in the past, but it was hit and miss these days.

When Jon's whining grew more insistent, she threw up her hands and gave in, giving him a second snack so that she could go back to her task in peace and quiet. Jon, never sure when his mother would give in to a second snack or not, had become unwilling to back down because he knew there was always a chance she would cave. By being more consistent in enforcing the 1-snack rule, Bethanne can help Jon to realize that whining won't help him to accomplish his goals and reduce this misbehavior in the future.

2.   *Not enough limits.* Positive parenting is not the same as permissive parenting. While it's important not to set expectations too high, it's equally important that children be given age-appropriate rules and boundaries to provide structure to their lives and help them learn control and emotional self-regulation. Not having enough limits can make it more difficult to enforce the few that you do have, as children will be used to getting their own way. They will also be missing out on the teaching opportunities and chances to practice self-regulation that healthy limits provide.

3.   *Forgetting to model.* As parents, we are being watched by our little ones all the time. How we respond to stress, the way we handle conflict, and the behaviors that we engage in around the home are all subject to notice by our children. Setting a good example and modelling the behaviors that we want our children to learn lends integrity to our discipline efforts and helps to normalize

good behavior for our children.

4.   It also builds trust, as they are unlikely to believe us when we say that a given behavior is important if we are neglecting that behavior ourselves. Children learn by watching as well as doing, so setting a bad example can easily lead to more frustration for us as parents as we have to deal with our children engaging in the same undesirable behaviors they have seen in us.

5.   *Unrealistic consequences or poor follow through.* Martin, a stay-at-home dad, became frustrated with his daughter Kelli when she refused to come back to the car after playing at the park. He tried several positive parenting technics to no avail, and then finally threatened to leave her behind if she didn't come now. Kelli thought for a moment and then ran back to the slides, content to be left to play. Exasperated, Martin had to retrieve her from the slides and start the whole problem over again. Stating a consequence that you can't actually follow through on ultimately undermines your authority and influence as a parent. The same holds true of failing to follow through on more realistic consequences.

6.   *Not enough quality time.* Building a good relationship is a vital component of positive parenting. Children need to feel loved, wanted, and valued. Spending quality time with your children can help to meet these needs, reducing anxiety and potential conflict or misbehavior.

7. *Unrealistic expectations.* As mentioned previously, it's imperative that the behavioral expectations you set for your children are age-appropriate. Expecting a three-year-old to act like a nine-year-old will only frustrate both of you and lead to repeated failure and anxiety.

8. *Not empathizing.* Acknowledging your child's feelings is another key component to positive parenting. Remember, acknowledging is about empathy, understanding, and respect – not about permissiveness or prioritizing emotions at the expense of teaching healthy boundaries. Instead, use empathy as a component in your teaching process.

9. *False praise.* In their attempts to be positive, many parents make the mistake of over-praising their children. While recognizing good behavior and praising accomplishments is important, it should always be done authentically. Children often pick up on false praise, and they know when they are being praised for something that they didn't really do well on. For example, if your child does a poor job picking up her toys because she was in a hurry to get on to another activity, don't tell her she did a great job. Instead, try expressing appreciation for her effort while acknowledging that she didn't do as well as she knows she can.

10. You might say something like, 'Ani, I appreciate that you picked up some of your toys. Why don't you come take a look with me and we'll see if they're all done?'

11. Praising your child for things that they didn't really accomplish or do well at makes praise less meaningful and effective in the long run. It's also helpful to focus praise more often on what your child has done (such as showing kindness to a sibling or picking up toys without being asked), rather than traits (such as being smart or pretty).

Chapter 7: Alternatives to Punishment

Punishment often seems like the quickest, most effective way to put a stop to misbehavior. In some cases, it may be necessary to resort to gentle, developmentally appropriate punishment to help children learn. However, most of the time effective alternatives to punishment can be found with a little thought and foresight. Let's take a look at some alternatives to punishment that can aid in positive parenting:

1. *Use natural consequences.* One way to help children learn the value and logic of good behavior is to allow natural consequences to occur. If your child becomes angry and knocks over his cup of milk, don't refill it. If she throws a toy and it breaks, don't rush out and buy her a new one. Instead of heaping an arbitrary punishment on

top of the misbehaviour and its consequence, use natural consequences as teaching opportunities.

2. *Meet needs.* If the misbehaviour has occurred due to an unmet need, help your child to express their need in a more effective way, then meet the need. Help them to recognize which modes of expression will help them to get their needs met and make a plan for the future. If the misbehaviour has created a mess or other situation that must be cleaned up, help them to take care of it, but don't do the work for them.

3. *Take a time out together.* Go on a walk, take a short trip to the park, or even just sit down and read a book together. Give your little one reassurance of your love and be their partner in success by experiencing the time out with them. Help them to see the timeout as a coping strategy for dealing with stress and frustration, and encourage them to choose to 'take a break' of their own when they feel themselves getting upset.

4. *Whisper.* If your child is upset or angry, whispering may catch their attention and distract them long enough for you to identify the root problem and implement a non-punitive solution.

5. *Offer choices.* If your child refuses to do something you've asked, give them the opportunity to make a healthy choice. In general, it's best to stick with just two alternatives. For example, if your child begins to argue when you ask them to turn off the TV, you can gently but firmly say something like, 'TV time is finished. You can either clean up your room or help me make dinner. Which one would you like to do?'

Regardless of the fact that discipline and boundaries are for a child's own health and well-being, they can nevertheless represent a loss of control when a child is asked to start or stop doing something that they don't want to. Offering choices can help them to feel more in control while still enforcing the boundary.

6.   *Problem-solve.* When a child misbehaves, instead of handing out punishment, encourage them to pr-oblem solve! For example, when four-year-old Laurel's brother Tyson grabbed a stuffed bear from her, Laurel reacted by letting out a shriek and beginning to hit Tyson. Her mother, Bella, stepped in to stop the hitting and take advantage of a teaching opportunity. She gently separated the two children and took the bear from Tyson before asking Laurel if yelling and hitting Tyson had helped her to get the bear back. When Laurel said no, Bella asked her daughter a key question: 'What might have worked better?' By asking Laurel, and later Tyson, what they could have done differently to accomplish their goals, Bella is helping her children learn to problem-solve difficult situations for themselves and think through the natural consequences of their actions.

Chapter 8: Tying It All Together

Well Supermoms, we've covered a lot of useful information in this section of the book! Parenting is truly one of the greatest challenges you will ever take on, but it can also be one of the most rewarding. We hope that this book will help you as you navigate the ups and downs of childhood while guiding your little one towards becoming a healthy, functioning adult.

As you experiment with the strategies in this book, keep in mind that positive parenting is a perspective. Cultivating a positive home environment, good communication, and a healthy parent-child connection are the first steps towards success. From there, don't be afraid to try different technics until you find what works. Your child's needs will change as he grows, and you can keep coming back to this book for new strategies to try at every developmental stage.

A nice perk of positive discipline is that it makes parenting more enjoyable for you, too! Although it may take a little more patience and conscientious effort than some other parenting methods, the effectiveness of positive parenting at reducing misbehavior and frustration is well worth the effort. Creating positive relationships with your children can lead to greater enjoyment and fulfillment for you as a parent as well.

We hope that you find the strategies in this book useful as you seek to connect, communicate with, and discipline your children in positive, growth-promoting ways. This guide is a great place to get started with positive parenting, and we hope you'll keep it handy as you move through the coming weeks, months, and years of childhood discipline. Read on to dive deeper into discipline at one of the most crucial stages of your child's life – toddlerhood.

Part 2

Toddler Discipline: The Ultimate Child-Raising Challenge for Supermoms

Introduction

Welcome to Part 2 of this book. Here, you will find your Ultimate Guide to Toddler Discipline.

Toddlerhood is an exciting time. Your baby is gaining an important sense of self, exploring her identity, learning to make decisions, discovering likes and dislikes, and hitting important milestones in language, cognitive, and social development.

As your baby moves into toddlerhood, it may at times seem that your little one has gone from adorable, cooing infant to overly emotional, unpredictable tyrant overnight. With terms like 'the terrible twos' coming into play, it's no wonder that many new parents feel overwhelmed during this stage of their baby's development.

However, there's no need to fear! Although the toddler years can sometimes be frustrating for both toddlers and moms, it's also an exciting time full of growth and fun.

Your relationship with your baby will deepen in new and enjoyable ways as you experience the ups and downs of emerging selfhood together. Positive discipline can help you navigate this special time effectively and with minimal frustration.

As your toddler begins to exert independence in his interactions with you and others, helping him to develop discipline will become vital to his success individually and socially. The toddler years are an important time for you to lay groundwork for skills in emotional regulation and social interaction, as well as instill behaviors that will set your child up for success as he prepares to enter the school years.

Some of the questions that will be answered in this section include:

- How does brain development relate to toddler discipline?
- What kinds of limits does a toddler need or not need?
- How can you develop healthy communication patterns with your little one?
- What are the best ways to help toddlers learn to deal with conflict?
- What discipline strategies are most effective in helping toddlers through this crucial stage of development?
- How can you as a Supermom stay calm in the face of toddler frustration?

As you move through the book and the answers to these questions, you'll find numerous tips and tricks to help you apply what you learn in real-world situations. You'll also discover that we've included insights from a variety of perspectives, because when it comes to toddler discipline, there is no such thing as 'one size fits all.' Each and every toddler has unique needs and temperament, so it's important to find the strategies that work for *your* child. The Supermom Series is here to help you do just that.

Let's get started!

Chapter 9: Brain Development and Why It Matters

Your child is growing quickly between 1 and 4 years of age, but not just in height and weight. When it comes to toddler discipline, it's crucial to gain a basic understanding of how your little one's brain and character are blossoming. Throughout toddlerhood, your baby will progress through important steps in both of these areas of development.

Developmental factors will play a direct role in what kinds of behaviors you might expect to see from your child. They will also impact how you respond to unproductive behaviors over time and how you help your toddler to learn the skills and self-regulation needed to grow into healthy, happy, functioning individuals.

Child development is an exciting and growing field of study. An in-depth look at all of the fascinating aspects of toddler brain development is outside the scope of this book, but a basic understanding of what's going on in your child's mind at different ages will help you to make the best decisions about how to interact with and encourage your little one's growing sense of independence.

Knowing what to expect and why certain behaviors happen will also help minimize your own frustration when baby 'misbehaves.'

In the following section, we will touch on some of the most important developmental achievements as they relate to toddler discipline from ages 1-4. However, don't worry if your toddler hasn't checked off every item in every category; each child develops at his or her own pace and may reach certain milestones faster or slower than the 'average' toddler. If you are concerned, or if your toddler seems particularly behind her peers, always consult a pediatrician to make sure that everything is on track.

12-18 Months: During this time, your toddler will begin to use the word 'no,' as well as make requests and follow simple, single-step instructions. She has little, if any, in the way of impulse control or emotional self-regulation. With her newfound mobility, she will begin to venture out and explore her environment on her own, although she will usually still need the reassurance of mom's presence. As she begins to assert her independence by expressing her wants and engaging in more independent activity, gentle discipline strategies will help her to stay safe and healthy.

The table below summarizes key milestones in brain and social/emotional development:

	Brain Development	Social/Emotional Development
by 12 – 18 months	- Expresses 'no' - Expresses desire (i.e. through pointing) - Recognizes everyday concrete objects such as bottles, blankets, and books - Can follow single-step verbal commands such as 'sit down' or 'come here.'	- May begin to have temper tantrums - May begin to show a fear of strangers - Shows affection for others - May cling to mom, especially around strangers or in unfamiliar situations - Uses pointing to share interesting finds with others - Begins to explore by venturing out alone, usually as long as a caregiver/ parent is present

18 Months – 2 Years: Your little one is well into toddlerhood. By now, he is starting to speak in short sentences, show an increased interest in other children, engage in simple imaginative play, and follow more complex instructions. He can also recognize the names of objects or pictures of objects and point to them when prompted. By this age, he is able to experience the full range of emotions.

Thanks to his burgeoning independence, more fully developed emotions, and lack of impulse control or emotional regulation, tantrums and refusals will begin to occur. Discipline strategies will continue to be focused on keeping your toddler safe and healthy, while helping them to develop self-control. Check out the table below for a more in-depth look.

	Brain Development	Social/Emotional Development
by 2 years	- Points to things or pictures when they are named - Able to form short sentences (2-4 words) - Begins to be able to sort basic shapes and colors - Begins to play rudimentary make-believe games - Can follow instructions with two steps	- Mimics the words and behavior of others - Gets excited when around other children - Increases in independence - Shows defiant behavior - For the most part, plays next to other children rather than with them, but is beginning to include other children in simple games such as chase

2-3 Years: By now, your toddler is exhibiting increasingly complex cognitive abilities, including following more complicated instructions and completing simple puzzles. He is also able to hold short conversations with full sentences and demonstrates enjoyment of and empathy for others. He's grown more socially independent, separating from parents with greater ease

The terrible twos have arrived full force, and you can expect more resistance when your toddler is tired or doesn't get his or her way. As with all stages of toddlerhood, discipline will continue to focus on health and safety, but now you can begin to introduce more concrete life skills such as sharing, turn taking, and better emotional regulation.

	Brain Development	Social/Emotional Development
by 3 years	- Can follow instructions with 3 steps - Can hold a short conversation using 2 to 3 sentences - Can play with more complicated toys that include moving parts - Engages in imaginative play with people and toys - Can complete very simple puzzles	- Copies the behavior of others - Shows affection for others - Engages in turn-taking during games and other activities - Shows concern for friends or family in distress - Understands possession ('mine' vs 'his' or 'hers') - Shows a wide range of emotions - Able to explore comfortably without a caregiver's presence at least some of the time - May be upset or uncomfortable with changes in routine

3-4 Years: The skills that began to appear between 12 and 36 months will continue to develop, leading your toddler to be able to engage in more complex cognitive activities, such as memorizing nursery rhymes and beginning to conceptualize things like time and contrast. She may also show an awe-inspiring degree of creativity as she engages in imaginative play with herself, her toys, and others.

By now, she's probably learned a degree of self-control when it comes to emotional regulation and is having fewer/shorter tantrums. She's made strides in impulse control, although it's still very much a work in progress. She has also learned to meet basic behavioural expectations, such as not throwing food, not hitting, and cleaning up toys. During this stage of development, discipline will become more focused on helping your toddler to learn the foundations of critical life skills such as cooperation and conflict resolution.

Age	Brain Development	Social/Emotional Development
by 4 years	- Abel to recite simple songs and poems from memory - Abel to tell stories and make predictions in a story - Understands the concept of counting and may be able to count - Begins to understand the concept of time - Understands the concept of 'same' and 'different'	- Becomes increasingly creative with imaginative play - Enjoys playing with other children more than playing alone - Is able to cooperate with other children - Not always able to tell what's real and what's make-believe - Talks about likes and interests

As you can see, the toddler years are a crucial time for brain and social development. As your child moves through each stage of toddlerhood, there some important supportive and risk factors to keep in mind to ensure your little one's optimal brain and social development.

Supportive factors are environmental, situational, and interpersonal influences which contribute to and/or support healthy development. *Risk factors*, on the other hand, may have an unhealthy, detrimental, or damaging effect on your child's brain and social/emotional development.

The table below lists some of the supportive and risk factors to look out for. Supportive factors should be encouraged within the home and risk factors minimized or eliminated.

Supportive Factors	Risk Factors
- Responsive caregiver interactions (caregiver interprets and responds to toddler's emotions/needs in an accurate and timely manner) - Loving interactions - Hugs - Adequate nutrition - Healthy sleep - Time for safe exploration in a caregiver's presence - Structure and routine	- Lack of loving interaction from mother or primary caregiver - Invasive or unresponsive parenting - Too much 'screen time' - Poor nutrition - Poor sleep - Stress in the home - Abuse of the toddler - Abuse in the toddler's presence

Now that we've gone over some of the exciting developmental steps you can expect to see throughout toddlerhood, it's time to move on to the next aspect of our discussion on toddler discipline: Limits!

*developmental tables adapted from information found at www.cdc.gov/ncbddd/actearly/milestones/index.html

Chapter 10: Toddlers Need Limits! Or Do They?

Your baby's mobility has opened a whole new world of exploration and experience. She will begin to take initiative, make requests, and experiment within her environment. As your toddler begins to make her needs and wants known in increasingly insistent ways, an important question arises: Just how much should you give your baby what she wants?

When Jessa, age 30 months, repeatedly refused to pick up her toys before snack time, her mother Karen was at a loss. The tantrums that erupted anytime Karen insisted that Jessa help clean up the mess before having a snack were exhausting. Karen finally started just handing out the snack first and then cleaning things up herself, rather than having to deal with her upset toddler. She knew Jessa was capable of picking up the toys, and she wanted to help her learn. But it was easier and less stressful to pick up the toys herself.

Karen's is a familiar conundrum for most of us. The truth is, setting limits can be difficult—even exhausting—for parents.

Why Set Limits

The time you spend helping your toddler to learn age-appropriate limits and boundaries is time well spent. Not only will healthy limits make your life easier in the long run, they are also a vital part of your little one's development. There are many benefits to setting healthy limits for your toddler, including:

Limits provide structure. Limits provide added structure and order to a toddler's world by helping her to know what to expect in different situations. Much as routine helps toddlers by lending predictability to their world, limits give toddlers the comfort of knowing what is expected of them.

Limits promote success. When there are no limits, toddlers encounter failure far more often than is necessary for growth. Allowed to run rampant, unregulated impulses, emotions and behaviors will lead to stress and conflict as the toddler attempts to interact with others and with their environment.

Limits give toddlers more opportunities to succeed by teaching them appropriate, successful behaviors for various situations. For example, teaching a child not to hit when they are angry will protect them from being hit back and keep conflict at a more manageable level, protecting their playtime and their relationships.

Limits boost confidence. As your toddler learns to achieve her goals within the healthy limits you've set for her, she will experience an increased sense of confidence in her own choices and abilities. Thanks to limits, she will begin to see cause and effect between behaviors that don't work and behaviors that do. Her growing understanding will help her to make sense of the world and her ability to make choices within it.

Limits provide teaching opportunities. It can be hard to set limits after a long day. In the moment, it is often faster, easier, and less stressful to give in to a toddlers' demands or let them get away with things that you'd rather not. However, setting limits is about more than just reinforcing good behavior. Each time you set a limit with your toddler, you have the opportunity for a teaching moment. For example, helping children learn to try the food on their plates is also an opportunity to teach them about the importance of keeping an open mind, appreciation for those who do kind things for us, and developing our likes and dislikes.

Limits prepare toddlers for the 'real world.' As toddlers grow into children, they will be faced with all of the expectations and consequences that come with social interaction in a community. Learning to regulate their emotions, follow instructions, and work with others will help them to succeed as they venture out into the school and community.

Limits keep toddlers safe. In some cases limits are necessary to ensure your little one's safety. For example, teaching toddlers not to climb up bookshelves or dig in the trash will help them to avoid accident or illness.

Limits keep toddlers healthy. In a modern world where far too many of us face the diseases of civilization, limits can help keep toddlers healthy. It can be tempting to give in to a 3-year-old's demands for ice-cream and cookies, but by setting limits on these types of unhealthy foods, you can help your toddler learn to self-regulate his food choices.

Limits help toddlers learn to socialize. Once toddlers start interacting with other children, they will need to engage in social behaviors such as sharing, turn-taking, resolving conflicts, and listening. Setting limits will help your toddler learn to socialize in ways that lead to healthy, enjoyable relationships and successful social interactions.

Why Toddlers Push Limits

You've chosen the most developmentally appropriate, growth promoting limits possible. You've carefully considered which ones are really necessary and are being careful not to over-restrict. You've set up and consistently enforced the limits as lovingly as possible…so why does your toddler keep pushing?

The short answer is, it's normal! Even the most skilled gurus of toddler discipline cannot eliminate push-back, nor should they—testing boundaries is an important part of your toddler's development. Sometimes, pushing back is indicative of a problem, but usually, it's simply normal toddler behavior.

Toddlers lack both impulse control and much ability to regulate their own emotions. Combine these facts with the intense ups and downs of emotion that most children experience, and it becomes a little easier to understand why they sometimes (or often) have difficulty resisting the urge to throw toys, hit a sibling out of frustration, have tantrums, or simply reach out and poke that one thing you've told them repeatedly not to touch.

It can't be stressed enough how important it is not to take these behaviors personally. Pushing back on boundaries is not only normal, your toddler truly can't help it much of the time. Self-control is an ever-evolving process, and will only come with time, love, and learning. Taking pushback personally adds unnecessary stress to a parent's life and limits opportunities for effective teaching.

There are a number of reasons why your toddler may push limits. Being aware of them can help us to maintain perspective in the more frustrating moments and deal with them more effectively. Let's take a look at some common reasons behind pushing back.

Experimentation. In the beginning, a toddler may not be convinced that she's *really* not allowed to climb up on the piano. Her repeated attempts to do what you've told her not to could be just plain old fashioned experimentation. '*Will mommy stop me this time? What about this time? What about if I try it while she's cooking? What about now?*' In these situations, staying calm, firm, and most of all consistent will help your toddler realize that the rule is not going to change.

In need of help. None of us like feeling tired, hungry, stressed, or overwhelmed. As adults, we've developed a variety of coping mechanisms to deal with these conditions, but your little one is still learning how to face the difficulties of life as a human. Sometimes, pushing on limits is the result of your toddler needing help and not knowing how to ask for it.

Just as you would take a moment to check your baby's diaper or hunger and thirst levels in response to crying, it's a good idea to take a moment and check in with your toddler's physical and emotional condition if they're pushing limits— especially if they also seem grumpy and out of sorts. In these situations, pushback can often be reduced or even eliminated simply by taking care of an unmet need.

Reassurance. Sometimes, toddlers need to be reassured that parents are reliable and that the world as they know it can be trusted to behave as expected. They push limits because they want to know that we will respond in predictable ways.

Teasing and play. Toddlers love to play, giggle, and have fun. Sometimes, they push limits simply to tease and laugh, or because they think it's a game. This behavior can occur on its own, but it can also be the result of mixed signals from a caregiver. Although toddlers can sometimes misbehave in the most adorable ways, giggling in response to cuteness when toddlers push limits can give the impression that misbehavior is a game.

For example, when 2-year-old Marie hit a friend during play, her mother Lisa, who was sitting with the children, said, *'No Marie. We don't hit.'* Marie teasingly slapped Lisa's knee in response. The mischievous grin and good humor on Marie's face caused Lisa to smile in amusement. Enjoying the attention, Marie slapped her mother's knee again. Not wanting to take away from her daughter's good mood, Lisa continued to say *'No, we don't hit'* even as her facial expressions and body language said *I like what you're doing.*

If you find yourself stuck in such a cycle while trying to set a limit, you can get things back on track by using clear body language that matches your intent. In this case, Lisa took Marie's hands in her own and made eye contact. Then, with a neutral expression on her face, she shook her head no and said, *'That's enough. We don't hit, okay?'* and waited for Marie to nod before letting go.

Attention. When toddlers feel ignored or unimportant, they often act out for attention. One way of doing this is to push limits. Sometimes, simply scooping them up for a moment of cuddle time or a story is all they need to get back to normal.

Love. Hand in hand with the need for attention is the need to feel loved. If your toddler is pushing back, he may simply need the reassurance of a hug and the knowledge that you love him. Don't be afraid to tell him often how much you care about him.

Tips for Setting Limits

So just how does one go about setting effective limits? The following tips will help you to set limits in ways that encourage growth and avoid authoritarianism.

Tip 1: Be consistent. When you set a boundary, be prepared to enforce that boundary on a regular basis. Boundaries that are firmly enforced one day and irrelevant the next hold little meaning for a toddler. By being consistent, your toddler will learn to respect the limit more quickly. He will also benefit from the structure and predictability that consistently enforced boundaries provide.

Tip 2: Know when to say yes. I know, we just said that it's important to be consistent. However, there will occasionally be times when it's appropriate or necessary to make an exception to a boundary or limit. For example, if your toddler is usually allowed one popsicle/day, a sore throat may make room for an extra. Knowing when to say yes shows your toddler that limits are important for our lives because they reasonable, not because they are arbitrary.

Tip 3: Use limits wisely. Toddlers are naturally scientists, exploring and experimenting with the world around them nearly every waking moment. They are constantly learning, discovering, and formulating. The ability to engage in these activities as they make independent choices is vital to their development and happiness. While some limits contribute to a toddler's development, too many restrictions can be just as detrimental as none. Limits should promote health, safety, social development, and emotional regulation without overly restricting the toddler's ability to play, explore, and make choices.

Tip 4: Be firm but gentle. Being too passive communicates to your toddler that you're not really serious about the limit being set, or that you don't care. Explain the limit in simple, age-appropriate language, in a firm but gentle tone while making eye contact. Don't become aggressive or be overly passive or distracted while setting limits.

Tip 5: Listen. Limits will sometimes cause frustration for your child. Listen to their frustrations, validate them, be willing to explain the purpose of the limit, and be prepared to help them navigate limits with distractions and alternatives. By listening and responding with care and consideration, you will teach your toddler that you are their partner in success.

Approaching limits with positivity and love will help you get the most out of them. When limits are set effectively, they do far more than just enforce desirable behavior. They also help your toddler to develop important self-regulation skills, provide a physically and emotionally safe structure in which to explore, and develop both confidence and self-awareness. Maintaining limits can be challenging, but investing the time and energy to do so will save you frustration down the line and set your toddler up for success in the coming school years.

Chapter 11: Communication is Vital

Communication is key in any relationship, and the one you have with your baby is no different. The period from ages 1 through 4 is vital to your toddler's emerging language and social skills. Parent-child communication during this stage of development is all about effective interaction, modelling communicative behaviors, and fostering confidence, safety, and self-development.

The first thing to remember about communicating with your toddler is that it is a *dynamic, two-way interaction*. One reaches out, the other responds. As you and your toddler learn to interact in increasingly responsive and effective ways, he will develop an increased sense of safety, confidence, empathy, and self-determination.

Let's consider some of the key components of effective communication.

Effective Communication: Talking

The way that a parent speaks communicates much more than simply words. When you engage verbally with your toddler, you are modelling how a conversation works, including important skills such as listening, empathy, and turn-taking. As toddlers observe you talking to themselves and others, what they learn about human interaction contributes to their understanding of what it means to communicate effectively and exist in a social context.

But setting a good example isn't the only thing to keep in mind. The way that parents speak to their toddlers also impacts how effective the communication is (does the toddler understand in a way that is actionable?) and the toddler's developing emotional and social understanding.

Talking to your toddler in ways that are too aggressive or too passive can have negative consequences on their emotional and social development as well as detract from the potential benefits of teaching moments and healthy discipline. Rather, parents should speak firmly but kindly as they seek to communicate with their toddlers.

With these key points in mind, let's consider some important tips for talking in ways that your toddler can understand:

Tip 1: Use eye contact. When talking with your toddler, don't expect them to listen or understand if you're really just talking *at* them. Set aside any distractions, make eye contact, and let yourself connect fully with your little one. Eye contact will help your toddler to pay attention to what you're saying and stay engaged in the conversation. It will also help bolster their sense of personhood by making it clear that you are interested in them.

Tip 2: Speak to them by name. Using your toddler's name while talking with them is another way to keep them focused on the conversation and give them a sense of importance as a co-communicator. It's especially good to use names when validating or when you're trying to let them know that you approve or disapprove. For example, *'Wow Jonny, that sounds so frustrating,'* or *'I love how you shared with your sister, Alex,'* or *'We don't throw food David—please stop.'*

Tip 3: Don't yell. Once you start yelling, chances are that your toddler's behavior will become worse, either right then and there or manifested the next day or week. Yelling sets a poor example for your toddler and is likely to cause them stress that could become damaging. You may also frighten them, further adding to their anxiety and fueling further misbehavior as they try to cope. Instead, speak in a calm bit firm voice. If needed, take a moment to breathe and calm down before speaking.

Tip 4: Be assertive, but not aggressive. As was discussed in the limits chapter, sometimes kids misinterpret our responses and may not realize that we are serious about a limit, or may think that we are engaging in play. Be clear about the purpose of your communications by using an assertive tone and body language when appropriate. However, do not mistake assertiveness for aggression. Assertiveness effectively communicates ideas and expectations, aggressiveness communicates danger, fear, and dislike.

Tip 5: Smile. Babies and toddlers are particularly responsive to facial expressions. As you no doubt discovered during the first year, sometimes a well-directed smile is all that it takes to brighten up a discontented baby. The same holds true for toddlers. Offering smiles during a conversation lets your toddler know that you enjoy talking with them and that the conversation is meant to be fun.

Tip 6: Minimize the use of 'no.' While some limits will certainly focus on what your toddler *should* do, many will be focused on what they should *not* do. Hearing 'no' over and over again throughout the day can be exhausting for your little one. Try to talk to him in positive terms that model reasoning. For example, instead of saying *'No Michal! Don't throw your food,'* you might try *'Hmmm, throwing our food makes the floor really sticky. Let's try saving it for later instead.'*

Tip 7: Don't talk too much. When speaking, keep it simple. Toddlers have short attention spans, and talking too much will likely cause your toddler to lose interest. For example, one day 2-year-old Jimmy threw his toy car straight at the window in his bedroom. His mom responded by saying, *'Now Jimmy, you can't throw your toy car at the window because if you end up breaking the window we're going to have to buy a new one, and that costs a lot of money, and besides, throwing things is dangerous—what if you hurt someone? How do you think it would feel? Do you think it's nice to...'* at this point, Jimmy has stopped tracking. His mother is using too many words, discussing people that aren't even present, and speaking in terms that a 2-year-old can't follow or relate to. Instead, she might say something like *'Jimmy, don't throw your toys in the house. Throwing is for outside.'* At two years of age, short, direct explanations of not more than 2-3 sentences are the most likely to result in understanding.

Tip 8: Use good manners. Using 'please' and 'thank you' will model good manners for your toddler, as well as help her to see that kids and adults alike deserve respect in conversation.

Tip 9: Ask questions. Asking open-ended questions is a great way to show interest in your toddler and encourage their participation in the conversation. When trying to encourage interaction, avoid questions that can be answered with a short yes/no. Instead of asking, *'Did you go to the park with Grandma?'* ask, *'What did you do at the park?'*

Tip 10: Don't limit conversation to directions. Finally, don't just use talk to give your little one directions or feedback. Their language skills are growing a mile a minute at this age, and they are learning that language can be used for all kinds of purposes. Support this growth and create positive interaction patterns by asking them about their day, their opinions, asking them to tell stories, solve problems out loud, etc. Responses will be limited at first, but need not be any less enjoyable. You will be astounded by how quickly your toddler's language develops in just a few short years.

Effective Communication: Listening

Listening goes hand in hand with talking. It's difficult to do one effectively without the other. Being a good listener will encourage your toddler to talk and help them develop good communication skills. Remember, effective communication with your toddler is dynamic and interactive, which means modelling both talking and listening abilities.

Listening serves a number of communicative purposes, including gathering information, opening the door for empathy, building relationships, giving respect, and gaining perspective. Listening will help you to understand what is going on in your little one's mind and heart, letting you relate to them better as you help them solve problems.

Tip 1: Ask for details. When your toddler tells you about what happened at church or that her baby doll feels sad, show that you are listening by asking for more details. *What happened first? Second? Third? Why is the baby doll sad? How will you make her happy?* In addition to showing that you are listening and interested, such questions elicit new language and help your toddler to practice important cognitive functions such as recall, mental modelling, and problem solving.

Tip 2: Pay attention. In today's world, multitasking has become a way of life, even when it's unnecessary. To show your toddler that you're listening and engaged, set aside devices such as phones or tablets and give them your full attention.

Tip 3: Use active listening. Active listening refers to listening that is purposeful and fully engaged. During active listening, you are fully focused on what is being said. Body language cues, including eye contact, mirroring facial expressions, and an attentive posture all contribute to active listening. When you listen actively, your toddler will be more likely to feel that what they have to say is important, and they will be encouraged to speak more.

Tip 4: Be physically interactive. High fives, hugs, and gestures are all great ways to show that you are listening and interested in what your toddler is saying. Getting bodies involved will also make the conversation more engaging and meaningful.

Tip 5: Give unconditional love. Toddlers seriously lack in impulse control and often don't know how to express themselves in socially appropriate ways. They may speak out of anger and even say things like *'I hate you'* or *'You're ugly.'* Remember, don't take it personally! No matter how your toddler speaks to you or what the content of their message is, make sure that they always know that you love them, no matter what. Unconditional love creates a safe space in which toddlers are able to speak freely and make mistakes without fear of losing your love or affection. This freedom will do wonders for their language skills, confidence, and trust in you as a parent.

How to deal with "I don't want..."

We've heard it a thousand times: *no.* Or, *I don't want (insert activity/behavior/food choice here).* Although '*no*' can be frustrating, it's actually a healthy part of your toddler's development. Saying '*no,*' or '*I don't want to,*' is often a toddler's way of expressing autonomy and inserting power over his own life. It's important that phrases like '*I don't want --*' are acknowledged, even welcomed. When toddlers see that their thoughts and opinions are important and respected, their growing individuality and independence are supported.

However, acknowledging the '*no*' doesn't mean giving in to it! As parents, we must learn to acknowledge while still setting limits and teaching appropriate behavior. For example, if little Sarah says, '*No, I don't want to turn off the tv,*' we can validate her contribution to the communication by saying calmly, '*The tv is really fun, isn't it? Sometimes I wish we could watch it all day long. You must feel a little sad that it's time to turn it off.*' This can be followed up by reinforcing the boundary: '*But too much tv takes our time away from other fun stuff, so that's why we only watch it for a little while. TV time is over, but now it's time to get ready for dinner.'*

Using this method, your toddler may still continue to say no, may even throw a tantrum, but they understand that their feelings on the matter were worth listening to. This also helps them to realize that the limit was enforced for a definable reason that always exists, and not because mom didn't understand what they wanted.

After listening, acknowledging, and then reinforcing the limit, be prepared to call on your toolkit of discipline strategies to help your toddler transition to keeping the limit. In chapter 5, we will go over a number of such strategies that will help you navigate the *'nos'* and *'I don't want tos'* with less stress and more success.

Chapter 12: How to Solve Conflicts

As your toddler increases in independence and begins to exert her will on the world around her, she will inevitably experience conflict. Conflicts may occur with siblings, other children, and with adults—including yourself!

Helping your baby learn to manage conflict in safe and healthy ways is vital to his development. Many parents feel that toddlers aren't cognitively developed enough to learn how to solve conflicts, instead opting to solve conflicts for their toddlers whenever possible. While there will be times when the most safe or appropriate action is for you to take care of a problem from your position as caregiver, there will also be many times when conflicts are an opportunity for you to teach your toddler basic skills in self-regulation, communication, and social interaction that will provide a solid foundation for more complex situations in the future.

The best way to help toddlers learn how to handle conflict is to allow them to experience it safely, with guidance and support when needed. When done effectively, taking advantage of these teaching moments to help your toddler learn how to get along with others will contribute to her sense of self, improve her ability to self-regulate, increase her social awareness, and help her develop empathy.

The first step in helping toddlers navigate conflict is to be good examples of how to use effective communication and conflict resolution strategies ourselves. Toddlers who see parents yell, argue, become rude or mean, call names, slam doors, etc. are more likely to do those things. Modelling healthy and productive strategies for conflict resolution helps toddlers to develop healthier and more productive strategies themselves.

However, modelling goes beyond simple behavior. It's also a good idea to model thought processes in the moments surrounding conflict. For example, during a stressful encounter at the bank teller drive through window, one mother looked in the rearview mirror to see her toddler looking at her with wide eyes. Chagrined, she realized that she'd been more than a little short with the teller.

Before the teller returned to the window, mom pulled out a quick think-aloud strategy: *'Boy, it makes me a little mad that this lady can't help me,'* she said. *'But I should be kind so that we can figure out the problem together. I think I'll take a deep breath. Will you help me?'* She and her toddler took a deep breath together and when the teller returned, mom finished the transaction much more calmly. By using a think-aloud strategy, she was able to model positive thought processes that take place in the real-world conflict resolution.

As adults, we are often able to resolve conflicts without much help from others. But what about toddlers? How much should we help them solve conflict?

Toddlers, especially 3-year-olds, are quick to turn to mom to solve conflicts for them. Your response to these requests may range from complete intervention in the case of safety issues, to prompts and guidance as toddlers learn to handle conflict themselves, to being aware but hands-off as you let your little one try to solve the problem on his own.

As long as safety isn't an issue, a good rule of thumb is to let your toddler try to work it out on her own. Doing so will give her the experience needed to internalize successful conflict resolution strategies. However, as you move your toddler towards increased independence in handling conflict, you will still need to stay aware of the situation at hand and be ready to offer guidance in the skills, strategies, and coping mechanisms needed to stay safe, respect others, and reach her goals.

As you help your toddler learn to deal with conflict, keep the following tips and strategies in mind:

Take a break. Teach your child that sometimes, conflict can be made easier by taking a break to calm down. In the beginning, you can simply remove them from conflict situations that have escalated.

Tell them that they *'need a break to calm down'* and can come back when they're ready. Before they come back to the situation, make sure they understand why they took a break—to calm down. Later, you can move on to asking them, *'do you need a break?'* when emotions start to escalate, encouraging them to regulate their emotions with more independence. Eventually, they may even 'take a break' of their own accord.

Encourage 'I' statements. Teach older toddlers to express the problem from their own point of view, and to listen to the point of view of others. For example, *'I felt sad when you didn't want to color with me because I just wanted to color too. So I took your crayons to make you mad.'* Learning to clearly state and understand the problem will help your toddler understand where conflict has arisen from. It will also help him to become more aware of his own reactions. When the problem is clearly stated, you can encourage your toddler to think about alternative choices for dealing with the problem, whether it originated in himself or another.

Make apologies. Encouraging toddlers to apologize after a conflict has been resolved helps them learn to take responsibility for their actions. It can also help them to reset after some intense emotions. When your child is 1, they probably won't be making apologies of their own although you can model this behavior for them. When they are 2, apologies may consist simply of a single word: *'sorry.'* Once your toddler is three, you can usually start directing them towards more meaningful apologies that acknowledge what was done wrong and what will done be better next time.

Problem-solve. If your toddler comes to you asking for help with a conflict, you may want to encourage them to solve the problem themselves. Validate their feelings and ask open-ended questions to get them thinking about what they could do to resolve the conflict. For example, *'Wow, I understand that she took your toy. That sounds really frustrating. How could we get it back? How could we find a way to share?'* You might suggest compromise strategies or offer guidance, but try to let your toddler choose how to solve the problem. Afterwards, praise them for figuring it out themselves.

Step back. Allow your little one to solve her own conflicts whenever possible. Taking a step back will give him the opportunity to learn from experience. However, that doesn't mean that you aren't aware or active in keeping an eye on the situation. Be ready to offer guidance if needed, but try not to take over unless necessary.

Be safe. Not all conflicts are benign. Watch out for safety issues and intervene immediately if necessary. During the toddler years, you'll especially want to watch out for thrown objects, pushing, hitting, biting, etc. If emotions or behaviors escalate and become unsafe for anyone involved, you may need to remove your child from the interaction. Usually, you can stop things from reaching that point by being aware of the situation and intervening before it gets out of hand.

Acknowledge both sides. If your toddler and a sibling or another child come to you together for help resolving a conflict, don't take sides. Encourage each participant to share their feelings and come up with ideas for solving the problem. Even if one child is clearly in the wrong, make sure that both leave the interaction with their respect intact.

Chapter 13: Discipline Strategies

Much toddler discipline revolves around the use of positive and negative consequences. Positive consequences are used when you want your child to repeat a behavior, like when you want her to pick up her own toys every evening. Positive consequences include praise, rewards, and attention. They let your child know that you like what she's doing. Negative consequences, on the other hand, are used when you want your child to stop a certain behavior, like when you want to him to stop coloring on the walls. Negative consequences include ignoring, distraction, and time-outs. They let your child know that you do not like what he has done.

Let's take a look at some effective discipline strategies.

Ignoring: Sometimes, toddlers misbehave simply to get your attention. Ignoring your child's behavior will eventually help them realize that tantrums, yelling, and demanding are not effective ways to get their needs met. In many cases, simply ignoring your toddler while they are misbehaving in this way is enough to get them to stop.

When using this strategy, do not talk to or look at your toddler while the behavior is happening. Ignoring works best for tantrums, interruption, and whining. This strategy is best for ages 18 months and up.

Distraction: Distraction means to get your toddler to focus on something else. Once she is distracted, the unwanted behavior will stop by default. For example, if your toddler is crying for an extra treat after lunch, you might play a game, look out the window together and have her point at every animal she sees, or read a quick story together. This strategy works at any age of toddlerhood.

Natural consequences: Natural consequences are consequences that occur directly because of what we have done. For example, if your toddler gets angry and tears up her paper, she no longer has a paper to draw on. Sometimes, it's best to allow natural consequences to take place to help toddlers learn. However, natural consequences should not be dangerous. Always intervene if safety is at stake, and don't allow your little one to engage in behaviors that put them at risk for harm. This strategy is best for ages 2 and up.

Delay: Delaying may be used to promote good behavior or discourage unhelpful behavior. For example, you might say, *'When you've picked up your toys, we can read a story,'* or *'If we don't finish lunch soon, we'll have to wait until tomorrow to go outside.'* This strategy can work for toddlers ages 2 and up.

Removal of privileges: Removing privileges works best when what is removed is related to the behavior in questions.

For example, taking away a toy that was thrown across the room. In most cases, your toddler should be able to get the privilege back after a set period of time, so long as they have either demonstrated that they are able to behave differently or that they are ready to try again. This strategy works best for toddlers 2 and up.

Time-out: Time-outs give your toddler a chance to calm down. For a time-out to be effective, you should remove from toddler wherever he is misbehaving. Many parents find that having a specific place in the house for time-outs works best. The time-out area should be free of distractions and relaxing. For toddlers, time-outs need not be long; often 2-5 minutes is enough to change the behavior and help your little one switch gears. This strategy works best for toddlers aged 2 and up.

Social rewards: Social rewards are things like praise, hugs, and high-fives as opposed to material rewards such as candy. Social rewards tend to be more powerful in the long run because they make you and your toddler partners in success. They also help to build trust and emotional currency. This strategy works for all ages of toddlerhood.

Sticker charts: Formal reward systems, such as a sticker chart, can make things like picking up toys and eating lunch feel like a game. Sticker charts also help toddlers feel powerful as they watch their own progress. This strategy is most effective for toddlers aged 3 and up.

Toddlers have pretty short attention spans, so it's important to give consequences, whether positive or negative, right after a behavior has occurred. This way, they can remember what it is that you do or do not like and more easily make connections between the cause and effect of behavior and consequence.

Keep in mind that negative consequences should never be used punitively or handed out in anger. Negative consequences help to reduce unsafe or unhelpful behaviors, but are never intended to hurt or punish your toddler.

When using consequences to discourage unsafe or unhelpful behavior, the CDC recommends the following steps:

Step 1: Identify the misbehavior.
Step 2: Give a warning.
Step 3: Give a consequence.
Step 4: Tell them why.
Step 5: Go back to positive communication.

Step 1: Identify the misbehavior. By alerting your toddler to the misbehavior, you are reminding them of expectations and giving them the chance to choose to change the behavior on their own.

Step 2: Give a warning. A warning further reminds your toddler that the misbehavior will have consequences and provides motivation should they need help making the decision to stop.

A warning also encourages them to think about cause and effect in an actionable way.

Step 3: Give a consequence. The consequence should be proportionate to the misbehavior and the toddler's development, and should be aimed at helping the toddler to recognize that the behavior is not effective or desirable.

Step 4: Tell them why. Make sure that your toddler understands why the consequence happened, either at the time or immediately after. Help them to make connections between the behavior and the consequence.

Step 5: Go back to positive communication. Once the consequence is over, provide positive interaction in the form of talk, hugs, or help to 'try again.' This will reassure your toddler that you love them and you are helping them to learn so that they and/or others can stay safe and healthy. Always go back to being positive.

As you follow the strategies in this chapter, you'll find that your individual toddler responds better to some methods than to others. While these strategies are usually considered gentle and effective, if anything seems to cause your little one stress and anxiety beyond what is normal for their age, stop and try a different one.

Chapter 14: 10 Common Mistakes and How to Avoid Them

Every parent makes mistakes when it comes to child-rearing, and you will no doubt experience your share. However, mistakes need not be considered a disaster. Far from it, conscientious parenting will help to turn many mistakes into important learning experiences. Even so, it can be frustrating to realize that a thoughtful strategy has actually been making a discipline problem *worse*. Knowledge is power, so let's take a look at some of the most common toddler discipline mistakes and how to avoid them.

Giving in to whining. It's often tempting to capitulate when your toddler won't stop whining for that favorite treat or more time at the park. However, giving in only teaches your little one that whining is an effective tool for reaching goals.

It also lets them know that the limit which brought on the whining isn't actually that important—that mom is willing to forget it given enough requests.

Instead of giving in to whining, firmly but gently remind your toddler what the limit is and why it's in place. Use simple language and don't overexplain. If your toddler continues to whine, try distracting them with a different activity, ask for their help, or give them an interesting task to complete. If the whining still doesn't stop, acknowledge your child's feelings and enact a productive consequence. For example, you might say '*I'm sorry, but we're not going to stay outside right now because outside time is over. I can see that it's really disappointing, but whining isn't the right way to handle it. I'd like you to spend five minutes in your quiet place so that you can calm down.*'

Lying. Sometimes it's all too easy to tell a white lie to keep kids in line. My neighbor once told her little boy that the ice-cream truck played music when it was *out* of ice-cream! However, kids will eventually catch on—and when they do, you will lose emotional currency. Toddlers need to be able to trust that their parents are being honest about how the world works. Lying is a quick fix that will eventually catch up with us, and nixes many opportunities for children to learn the healthy skills needed to deal with reality.

Inconsistency. Another pitfall of guiding your little one through toddlerhood is inconsistency. The parental zeal you felt when you established a new routine or set a new limit on Tuesday may have given way to exhaustion by Friday—at which point it's all too easy to let the new structure slide. Her behaviors may become worse as she learns that she c an 'get away with it,' and she may experience stress from not knowing what to expect. Even though it can be challenging, try to remain as consistent as possible with toddler discipline. It will pay off in the long run for both of you.

Bribes. Bribery is often an effective short-term solution, and on occasion it may be your best course of action. However, bribery rarely teaches or reinforces underlying principles of behavior and citizenship that your toddle needs to develop. Bribery can cut short teaching opportunities that may have provided your toddler with valuable insight and helped them practice making positive choices. Whenever possible, try to motivate your little one with positive reinforcement (hugs, smiles, high-fives) and discipline rather than bribes. Doing so will help them to internalize the behaviors you are trying to teach and develop an understanding of why those behaviors are expected.

Talking too much. As amazing as your toddler's developing language abilities are, they aren't quite ready for drawn out or overly complicated explanations. Make sure to speak in simple, clear terms appropriate to your toddler's age. Over-explaining or talking too much can lead to boredom, tuning-out, or confusion, all of which may make discipline problems worse.

Poor follow-through. Sometimes, adults tell toddlers that they'll play with them 'later' or get them from their play room in 10 minutes when in fact, the adult is simply trying to appease the toddler so that they can get back to what their doing. However, this undermines your toddlers trust in your reliability. It's important to avoid making promises that you aren't able to keep.

Inconsistency can undermine your toddler's view of your reliability as well as the positive behaviors you are trying to teach her.

For example, if your toddler is insisting on a story during a particularly busy afternoon, it can be tempting to tell them *'sure, we can read the book in a little while,'* just to get them to stop asking. However, if you're not actually able to read the book later, it's better just to be honest.

Try saying, *'I know how much you love that book. I would love to read it together, but today is really busy. Let's read it tonight or tomorrow. Which one would you like?'*

Reacting. Reacting is far less effective than responding in most situations. If you find it difficult to step away from a reaction in a stressful situation, try building up your personal toolbox of strategies for dealing stress. Motherhood can be challenging, frustrating, and at times incredibly overwhelming. It's important to have healthy coping strategies to reduce frustration and help us to get back on track in difficult moments. Breathing, counting to 10, and calmly expressing our own feelings in non-aggressive ways can all be helpful in moving away from reacting. This will be discussed further in the next chapter.

Not enough expressions of love. We all express love in different ways. Some people grow up in families where hugs and I love yous were exchanged freely, while others used subtler ways to communicate their feelings. At one point in time, it was considered developmentally healthy to refrain from giving your toddler too many overt expressions of love, lest they fail to 'toughen up' against the realities of life. However, many years of research in child development has shown that toddlers need love to thrive. Make sure that your toddler knows that you love him, including through hugs, smiles, and words.

Chapter 15: Secrets of Staying Calm

It's no secret that parenting is hard. Between loss of sleep, constantly paying attention, tantrums, refusals, and what can feel like a thousand other spinning plates, it's inevitable that you will experience frustration as a parent.

However, for your own health and the health of your baby, it is helpful to learn how to remain calm in the face of toddler discipline problems. In this chapter, we will go over some important strategies to help you stay during your child's most frustrating moments. With this information in hand, you will be able to navigate the ups and downs of toddlerhood with more efficiency and fewer grey hairs!

Don't react, respond. When Marissa's 3-year-old son Alex got angry and knocked his bowl of spaghetti off the table, her first instinct was to start yelling. It had been a long week and she was near her wits end. As the spaghetti hit the floor, all she wanted to do was snap at her son, toss him in his room, and close the door without another word.

Alternatively, she could take a deep breath, remind him gently but firmly that throwing food on the floor was not okay, and put him in time out to calm down before helping him clean up the mess.

In the first case, Marissa would have been simply *reacting* to her son's behavior. Reactions are often only moderately predictable at best, and may be more about protecting our own emotional state than helping our toddlers learn. To simply react is to indulge our first impulse in the face of frustration. It's almost always better to *respond* to misbehavior than to react. In the second scenario, Marissa would first recognize that she was about to react, then give herself a give herself a second to breathe and make choices about how to handle the situation. Reacting takes away our parenting choices, while responding is all about those choices.

Remember that you're the one in control. When a toddler acts out in defiance or refuses to do as they're asked, it's not uncommon for a stressed parent to feel like the toddler is the one in control of the situation. Feeling out of control can be just as negative for parents as it is for little ones. Remembering that you are the one in control can help you to take a breath and re-evaluate before taking action.

Never take it personally. Yes, it is possible for parents to get their feelings hurt! When your two-year-old twists away from your hug with an angry '*No!*' or gleefully dumps out the box you just asked her not to touch, it can sometimes be tempting to take such behavior as a personal affront.

As your child learns to self-regulate, he will sometimes get mad at you, lash out in frustration, and may even say unkind things towards you. Taking these behaviors personally will only make it harder for you to identify and deliver the most effective responses and discipline strategies. If you find your emotions getting caught up in the drama, take a moment to step back and breathe or ask a partner to take over while you calm down. Maintaining perspective will help you to navigate your toddler's behavior with less stress and more success.

Count to ten. If you find yourself about to react rather than respond, have a sudden flash of emotion at the end of a long day, or simply need to control a giggle when your toddler misbehaves oh-so-cutely, take a moment to count to ten and let the impulses pass.

Don't try to 'fix' everything. Remember, you want to foster your toddler's ability to solve her own problems in healthy and constructive ways. This means sometimes taking a step back and offering encouragement instead of direct intervention. These strategies aren't just important for your toddler, they're also important for your own sanity. The parent who is constantly on guard, swooping in to fix every difficulty or conflict that arises, is more likely to experience stress, exhaustion, and burn out. She is also more likely to feel anxious that a toddler's 'mistakes' are her fault, instead of viewing them as exciting steps in the process of growth.

Be consistent. Consistency is an important parenting strategy, but it also benefits mom.

When you are consistent in your efforts to provide discipline, your toddler will likely experience less frustration and act out less over time, which means frustration for you as well. You can also feel good knowing that you are helping your toddler learn to be safe and productive.

Keep the big picture in mind. It can be easy to feel overwhelmed in some of the more difficult moments of toddler discipline. It can help to take comfort in remembering two things: First, *what you are doing matters.* Second, *toddlerhood doesn't last forever.*

Plan for breaks and 'me' time. Regardless of whether you're a full-time caregiver or juggling parenting and a career, it's important to plan time for yourself. By giving yourself breaks and time to relax, unwind, and get some needed mental space, you will return to your toddler with more to give. You will be able to experience the joys of parenting more fully and handle the frustrations more effectively.

Get enough sleep. Lack of sleep is a common issue faced by parents, even when babies become toddlers. If you find yourself struggling to get enough shut-eye, you might try setting up a play-group exchange that would allow you to get a couple of extra hours' nap time once or twice a week, or plan to take naps while your little one is sleeping. Although it can be tempting to stay up late to get things done, you may benefit from an earlier bedtime when possible. Having enough shuteye will make you more mentally alert and emotionally resilient.

Chapter 16: Tying It All Together

We've gone over some exciting information in this section! Toddlerhood can be a challenging but truly rewarding time with your little one. We hope that you will take what you've learned and use it to create an effective, healthy environment for your toddler to grow in.

Keep in mind that none of the topics covered in this book are meant to be treated in isolation. Each facet of toddler discipline works with the others—brain development influencing strategies, strategies creating a positive environment, a positive environment helping toddler and mom to stay calm, calmness creating a space for more effective strategies. Each aspect supports the others in an improved and increasingly effective whole.

As you move through the toddler years, you will need to experiment, adapt and try new things as your child's needs change. It's an exciting time of life, one that will definitely keep you on your toes as your toddler makes strides in cognitive development, language abilities, social interaction, and emotional intelligence.

Chapter 17: In Conclusion

We hope that this 2-in-1 guide to positive parenting has helped you to gain practical, applicable insights into positive parenting and toddler discipline. The pages of this book are meant to help you have a happy, fulfilling relationship with your child as you help them grow.

No matter the age of your child, there will always be challenges to address. There will always be new experiences that they must learn to navigate and competing priorities that they must learn to balance. Through positive parenting, you can experience the fulfillment that comes from watching your child grow in independence and selfhood as she learns to make healthy choices and navigate life's difficulties mindfully.

This book contains many effective techniques and strategies for applying positive discipline in your home, but even these are just a sampling of what's out there. As you try them out, don't be afraid to tweak them for your own unique situation and your own unique child. Again, if you're not sure about trying a strategy or about your child's behavior, consult your pediatrician.

We recommend that you keep this book on hand as your child grows. As was mentioned earlier, a strategy that doesn't work now may be perfect when your child is a year or two older. Most of the principles in this book apply to teens as well, and many of the strategies can be adapted accordingly. Refer back to these pages whenever you need inspiration for an effective discipline technique, something new to add to your personal cool-down toolbox, or a refresher on the underlying principles of positive parenting.

So that's it Supermoms! We hope that you will find the insights, strategies and tips in this book helpful as you work to effectively teach your children positive behaviors, emotional regulation, and social skills. We also hope that principles you've explored here will make a positive difference in how you experience these amazing formative years. Although this time in your child's life can be challenging, it can also be immensely rewarding.

Just remember, *discipline is teaching moments delivered with love*. It need not be harsh to be effective. In most cases, harshness does not lead to desired outcomes in the long run. Positive parenting does take a little more patience, but it is by far less stressful than many punitive approaches. By reading this guide, you have taken the first step towards a successful and enjoyable experience with discipline for both your child and yourself.

Thank You for Buying My Book!

Your Free Gift

Funny Riddles for Children

https://supermomseries.wixsite.com/riddles

Download it now!

Can I Ask You a Favor?

If you enjoyed this book I would really appreciate it
if you would post a short review on Amazon.com.
I read all the reviews personally and your opinion is
extremely important for me.

To leave a review click
https://www.amazon.com/dp/B072NNVDJK

Made in the USA
Columbia, SC
21 October 2018